# Pray with Me Daddy

by
Robert Wolgemuth

Honor Books
Tulsa, Oklahoma

**2nd Printing**

*Pray with Me Daddy*
ISBN 1-56292-533-4
Copyright © 1999 by Robert Wolgemuth
330 Franklin Road
Suite 135-G
Brentwood, Tennessee 37027

Published by Honor Books.
P.O. Box 55388
Tulsa, Oklahoma 74155

# Introduction

Stop and think about what it truly means to pray. You and I, just ordinary people, walk boldly into the presence of the Almighty and Sovereign Creator and speak to Him as though He were our friend. Yet He not only gives us permission to do this, He invites us to come! Pretty incredible, isn't it? So here we are, standing in His Holy company, bringing our praise, our thanksgiving, and our concerns to Him. And there He is, listening to us like a loving father.

Now, if that weren't enough, His invitation isn't for us alone. He also loves to hear the prayers of our children and wants them to come along for this unbelievable experience.

This little book was created to help you and your daughter discover the wonder of entering God's awesome presence—together. My prayer is that *Pray with Me Daddy* will be an extraordinary journey for you.

# Contents

Protection . . . . . . . . . . . . . . . . . . . . . . . . . . . . . . . . . . . . . . . . . . .6

Conversation . . . . . . . . . . . . . . . . . . . . . . . . . . . . . . . . . . . . . . . .30

Affection . . . . . . . . . . . . . . . . . . . . . . . . . . . . . . . . . . . . . . . . . . .50

Discipline . . . . . . . . . . . . . . . . . . . . . . . . . . . . . . . . . . . . . . . . . . .74

Laughter . . . . . . . . . . . . . . . . . . . . . . . . . . . . . . . . . . . . . . . . . . . .94

Faith . . . . . . . . . . . . . . . . . . . . . . . . . . . . . . . . . . . . . . . . . . . . . .114

Conduct . . . . . . . . . . . . . . . . . . . . . . . . . . . . . . . . . . . . . . . . . . .138

About the Author . . . . . . . . . . . . . . . . . . . . . . . . . . . . . . . . . . . .159

The LORD is my light and my salvation—
whom shall I fear?
The LORD is the stronghold of my life—
of whom shall I be afraid?

PSALM 27:1

Darkness can be a pretty frightening thing. Even in our own house,
when it's completely dark, we walk slowly and carefully, hoping we
don't run into anything that would hurt us and really hoping that nothing
jumps out at us from the shadows. Our world can also be a dark
and frightening place with lots of reasons to be afraid.

God is our light. His presence cancels darkness. He shows us
where we are, and He lovingly helps us to see who we are, too.
There is no need to be afraid.

### Dad Prays

Thank You, Heavenly Father, for Your light. Thank You for the way Your light takes away my fear and gives me hope. Forgive me for needlessly living in the dark. Please wrap Your arms of assurance and confidence around my daughter today. Help her to live in Your light and to not be afraid. Amen.

Daughter Prays

Heavenly Father, thank You for Your light. Your light takes away
my fear and gives me hope. I do not need to live in the dark.
Help my dad remember that You are the reason for his safety
and success. Let Your light make him brave. Amen.

There is no one like the God of Jeshurun,
who rides on the heavens to help you
and on the clouds in his majesty.
The eternal God is your refuge,
and underneath are the everlasting arms.

**DEUTERONOMY 33:26, 27**

Have you ever seen a daddy standing in a swimming pool,
begging his frightened little girl to jump into his arms?
"I'll catch you," he says with confidence. "Don't be afraid."

What a great picture this is of our God. There is no one like Him.
He is so great that He can put a saddle on the heavens and
ride them like a pony! And He says to us, "Don't be afraid.
My arms are big enough to catch you when you jump,
or when you fall." I'm so thankful to know a God like that.

## Dad Prays

Thank You, Heavenly Father, for Your everlasting arms.

Thank You for Your promise to catch me when I fall.

Forgive me for not trusting You, thinking I can save myself.

Please help my daughter to feel Your protection. Help her to know

how truly great You are, especially when she's afraid. Amen.

### Daughter Prays

Heavenly Father, thank You for holding me in Your arms.
Thank You for catching me when I fall. I can trust You.
Help my dad to trust You and let You protect him, too. Amen.

He who dwells in the shelter of the Most High
will rest in the shadow of the Almighty.
I will say of the LORD, "He is my refuge and my fortress,
my God, in whom I trust."
For he will command his angels concerning you
to guard you in all your ways.

PSALM 91:1, 2, 11

There are two ways to be protected. One way is to build a building, complete with dead-bolt locks, bulletproof windows, and the latest in electronic surveillance. The other is to hire a security guard— someone who stays up all night, making sure that we are safe. God's protection of His children is so complete that He has done both. He has built a fortress around us, and He has assigned angels to stay awake around the clock. Because of what God has done, there is no reason to be afraid.

## Dad Prays

Thank You, Heavenly Father, for safety. Thank You for guarding our family. Forgive me when I forget that Your fortress and Your angels are there. Please help my daughter to know that even though I cannot always protect her, she can always feel safe because of You. There is no need to be afraid. Amen.

## Daughter Prays

Heavenly Father, thank You for keeping us safe.
My dad does not need to worry about us. You are strong,
and Your angels are always with us. Help my dad know
that we are all safe because of You. Amen.

$A$s for God, his way is perfect;
the word of the LORD is flawless.
He is a shield
for all who take refuge in him.

**PSALM 18:30**

When neighbor children argue with each other, sometimes they brag, "Oh yeah, well my daddy is bigger than your daddy." There is something in children that longs to have someone bigger and stronger to love them and protect them. This creates security for a little person.

Our God loves us and protects us. There is no storm that is too powerful, no danger that is too threatening, and no opponent that is too strong for our Father in Heaven. This creates security for little people and big people, even for men who are the biggest daddies in their neighborhoods.

### Dad Prays

Thank You, Heavenly Father, for security. Thank You for
the confidence that comes from knowing who You are. Forgive me
when I try to face the fears and troubles of this world without You.
Please help my daughter to remember that even when this dad fails,
You never fail. Amen.

### Daughter Prays

*Heavenly Father, it makes me feel good to know
that You are always with me. I do not have to be afraid.
Help my dad know that You are with him, too. Help him
to know that he does not have to face hard times alone. Amen.*

E*ven though I walk
through the valley of the shadow of death,
I will fear no evil, for you are with me;
your rod and your staff,
they comfort me.*

**PSALM 23:4**

"I think my dad loves the dog more than he loves me,"
the teenage girl said angrily, to the counselor at school. "When our dog
doesn't come home at night, my dad goes outside and walks the
neighborhood, yelling his name. When I stay out too late,
he doesn't know where I am and doesn't even care."

A good shepherd's protection includes both his "rod," the short stick
he uses to defend sheep, and his "staff," the long stick he uses
to help them up when they fall. God's guideance includes
strength and gentleness. These make us feel loved.

## Dad Prays

Thank You, Heavenly Father, for discipline and gentleness.
Thank You that, even though I often resist Your discipline,
it makes me feel loved. Thank You also for your gentleness.
Please help my daughter to understand that her security will
always include both toughness and tenderness. Amen.

**Daughter Prays**

Heavenly Father, thank You for being fair.
Thank you for a dad who loves me so much he provides
both discipline and gentleness. He wants to teach me
right from wrong. Amen.

I*f God is for us,*
*who can be against us?*

**ROMANS 8:31**

A group of students went to a very talented young woman and
asked her if she would be willing to run for class president.
They told her that she would be the perfect person for this job.
Then they said to her, "Every person at our school has promised us
that they will vote for you." If the girl would say, "Yes, I'll run,"
who would be able to defeat her? That's right, no one.

God loves us, He will always love us, and only His vote counts.
So, no matter how we may be feeling at this moment, with God on our side,
there is no need to be afraid. Isn't this a wonderful thing?

### Dad Prays

Thank You, Heavenly Father, for choosing to love me.
Thank You that I can know You love me, even when I don't feel You there.
Forgive me for forgetting that this will always be true.
Please help my daughter to live with the confidence of
Your love and not be afraid. Amen.

**Daughter Prays**

Heavenly Father, thank You for choosing to love me.
You love me all the time. I know that this is true.
Help my dad to know that You love him all the time, too.
He does not have to be afraid of anything,
no matter what happens. Amen.

Do not let any unwholesome talk
come out of your mouths,
but only what is helpful for building others up
according to their needs,
that it may benefit those who listen.

**EPHESIANS 4:29**

The words people speak can have a powerful effect on others. The Bible compares the tongue—where words come from— with the rudder of a great ship. Even though tongues and rudders are quite small, they both have a huge impact on people and boats.

We need to be sure that our words are good words, true words, and encouraging words. We want people to look forward to hearing us speak and not to be hurt by what comes out of our mouths.

## Dad Prays

Thank You, Heavenly Father, for giving us words.
Thank You for the way words have the power to help others.
Forgive me for the times when I have said unkind and hurtful words.
Please help my daughter to be a girl who builds up
her family and her friends with her words. Amen.

## Daughter Prays

Heavenly Father, thank You for giving us words.
Words can help people. Words can hurt people, too.
I need to watch what I say. Help my dad to remember how
important his words are at work and at play and at home. Amen.

I love the LORD, for he heard my voice;
he heard my cry for mercy.
Because he turned his ear to me,
I will call on him as long as I live.

**PSALM 116:1, 2**

I'd know your voice anywhere. No one sounds quite like you.
Even in a large crowd, when you call me, I recognize that sound.
It's familiar anywhere. Isn't it wonderful to know each other so well?

God knows the sound of our voices, too. When we call on Him,
He hears us. He's not too busy to listen—or to answer.
There are very few things more incredible than knowing that
the One who created the entire universe with His voice
stops what He's doing when He hears mine!

Dad Prays

Thank You, Heavenly Father, for listening. Thank You for loving me
enough to know the sound of my voice. Forgive me for not listening,
even to the voices of those I love. There are so many noises in
my daughter's life, so please help her to be attentive to
my voice and to Your voice, too. Amen.

### Daughter Prays

Heavenly Father, thank You for listening to me.
I am glad that You know the sound of my voice.
Help me to listen the way You do.
Help my dad listen to my heart as well as to my voice.
And help my dad listen to You. Amen.

Do not break your oath,
but keep the oaths you have made to the Lord. . . .
Simply let your "Yes" be "Yes,"
and your "No," "No."

**M A T T H E W   5 : 3 3 , 3 7**

When a person is going to be a witness in court, he puts his left hand on a Bible and raises his right hand, then he promises to tell the truth. Isn't it interesting that if everyone really did what they promised to do— to tell the truth—there probably would be no need to be in court at all?

Jesus made this very clear: When we talk, we must tell the truth. And when we make promises, we must keep them. If we fail to remember these things, we will spend our lives in lots and lots of trouble— guaranteed. The words we speak are very important.

### Dad Prays

Thank You, Heavenly Father, for promises.
Thank You that Your promises are sure. Forgive me for being
too casual about the words I speak and for forgetting my promises.
Please help my daughter to remember how important
it is to speak the truth, and give her the determination
to keep her promises. Amen.

**Daughter Prays**

Heavenly Father, thank You for keeping Your promises.
Help me to keep the promises that I make.
And help my dad to keep his promises, too.
His words mean a lot to me. Amen.

"Because he loves me," says the LORD,
"I will rescue him;
I will protect him, for he acknowledges my name.
He will call upon me, and I will answer him;
I will be with him in trouble,
I will deliver him and honor him."

PSALM 91:14,15

When a tennis player wants to improve her game, she usually takes a friend
with her who is good enough to hit the ball back across the net.
Imagine how hard it would be to improve at tennis if her friend
never returned the ball. When people talk to each other,
they need to learn to "hit" words back and forth like tennis balls.

Because God is the Master Communicator and because He loves us,
He understands how important it is to answer when we talk to Him.
He would never let all those "tennis balls" just fall at His feet.

## Dad Prays

Thank You, Heavenly Father, for answering me.
Thank You for listening when I talk to You, and
thank You for responding. Forgive me when I let the words
that people speak—especially the people I love—fall at my feet.
Please help my daughter to help me be a better
"tennis player" with words. Amen.

**Daughter Prays**

Heavenly Father, You listen to me when I talk.
Thank you. And thank You for answering me.
I want to try hard to be a good listener.
Please help my dad to be a good listener, too. Amen.

My mouth is filled with your praise,
declaring your splendor all day long.

**PSALM 71:8**

Grandparents love to show everyone pictures of their grandchildren.
We rarely have to beg them to show us the latest snapshots from their wallets
or their purses. And when we ask grandparents how their little ones are doing,
they can go on and on about all their accomplishments. It's so automatic
that sometimes we don't even have to ask!

When we go through the day, our conversations
with everyone ought to include wonderful things about God,
because we are so excited that we know Him. And it's only
natural that our love for Him would make us want to do this.

### Dad Prays

Thank You, Heavenly Father, for being in my life.
Thank You for filling my mouth with the excitement of knowing You.
Forgive me for the times when I don't love You like I should.
Please fill my daughter with so much love for You that
she tells her friends at school how wonderful You are. Amen.

## Daughter Prays

Heavenly Father, thank You for being in my life.
You make me so happy to know You.
I love You so much. Help my dad to be excited, too.
Help my dad to tell everyone about You. Amen.

Be kind and compassionate to one another,

forgiving each other,

just as in Christ

God forgave you.

**EPHESIANS 4:32**

A failing grade in school can be an awful thing.
It makes us feel terrible about ourselves, and sometimes it even
makes us resent our teacher. A bad grade reminds us of our failure.
Now can you imagine how relieved we would be if our instructor
would take an eraser and cancel our bad mark in her grade book?

God does that. Because of what His son, Jesus, did on the cross, our sins
are forgiven. And this gives us the privilege of forgiving others, too.
The Bible calls us to show kindness and compassion,
and in a family, it's a wonderful thing to do.

## Dad Prays

Thank You, Heavenly Father, for forgiveness.
And thank You for giving us the power to forgive others.
Forgive me for the times I hold onto the failures of others,
refusing to forgive them. Please help my daughter to feel
Your forgiveness and to know the happiness that comes
when she forgives others. Amen.

**Daughter Prays**

Heavenly Father, thank You for being kind to me.
You make me happy. I want my dad to be happy, too.
Sometimes people hurt my dad on purpose.
Help my dad to be kind to them. Amen.

$S$tore up for yourselves treasures in heaven,
where moth and rust do not destroy,
and where thieves do not break in and steal.
For where your treasure is, there your heart will be also.

MATTHEW 6:20,21

Almost every day there is a story in the newspaper that tells about
fires, floods, earthquakes, or robbers. As a result of one of these
terrible things happening, people can lose everything they own.
It can be a very sad thing.

Because God is love, He gives us the ability to love each other forever.
This is one of those "heavenly treasures" that no disaster will ever be able
to take away from us. No matter what happens, I will always love you,
and you will always love me. What a wonderful thing this is!

**Dad Prays**

Thank You for Your love, and thank You for giving me
a special love for my precious daughter that no one can take away.
Please fill my daughter with this kind of lasting love, too. Amen.

**Daughter Prays**

Heavenly Father, thank You for Your love.
It will last forever.
Thank You for giving me love for my dad.
No one can take it away.
Please give my dad this kind of love, too. Amen.

People were bringing little children to Jesus
to have him touch them. . . .
And he took the children in his arms,
put his hands on them and blessed them.

**MARK 10:13, 16**

Almost everyone loves to be touched. Little children, especially little girls, love it when their daddies hold their hands. Most teenagers like hugging. Even athletes smack each other when good things happen on the field. Grown-ups almost always shake hands to say "hello."

God understands how important touching can be. When Jesus saw the children coming to Him, He stopped what He was doing, and He held them. When He healed sick people, He tenderly touched them. We cannot forget how important touching is in our family.

### Dad Prays

Thank You, Heavenly Father, for touch.
*Thank You for Your example of loving people,*
*then touching them so they'd know for sure.*
*Forgive me when I'm too busy or when I forget to hold my girl.*
*Please help my daughter to remind me to be tender,*
*because sometimes dads forget. Amen.*

**Daughter Prays**

Heavenly Father, thank You for touching my heart.
That's when I know for sure that You love me.
I need to remember to touch my daddy's heart too.
I think he likes hugs the best.
Give my dad a tender heart like Jesus. Amen.

Praise be to the God and Father of our Lord Jesus Christ,
the Father of compassion and the God of all comfort,
who comforts us in all our troubles,
so that we can comfort those in any trouble
with the comfort we ourselves have received from God.

2 CORINTHIANS 1:3,4

Most dads are excellent lecturers. When it's time to teach
a lesson to his children or to make a point
when they have done something wrong, a dad can be the best.
And because most people learn by gathering helpful information,
this can be a good thing. But sometimes, lectures won't do.

God has plenty to say that instructs us. What would we do without
all the helpful information in His Word? But God is filled with
so much love and compassion that sometimes He comforts us
instead of lecturing us. Isn't it wonderful that dads
can learn this balance from their Father in heaven?

## Dad Prays

Thank You, Heavenly Father, for comforting us.
Thank You for knowing when to teach Your children
and when to just tenderly hold them.
Give me the wisdom to know what to say—and what not to say.
Please help my daughter to learn how to tenderly comfort
her friends when they are hurting. Amen.

### Daughter Prays

Heavenly Father, thank You for making me
feel better after bad things happen.
Thank You for forgiving me when I've done wrong.
Thank You that my dad is there to help.
I want to help others, too. Amen.

You are no longer foreigners and aliens,
but fellow citizens with God's people
and members of God's household.

**E P H E S I A N S   2 : 1 9**

Do you know what it's like to be the new kid at school?
No one knows who you are. No one even knows your name.
And sometimes it feels like everyone is staring at you.
This can be a pretty scary thing.

In God's family, no one is the "new kid."
We are all brothers and sisters, because we have the same
Heavenly Father. And not only does everyone know our name,
everyone loves us so much that they'd be willing to do anything for us.
God gives us this example of His family so we can know
what to do in our own family. Isn't that wonderful?

### Dad Prays

Thank You, Heavenly Father, for Your family.
Thank You for giving me a perfect example of being the father for our family.
Forgive me for treating others like they aren't my brothers and sisters.
Please help my daughter to remember how important family is to You
and to never treat anyone like a "new kid." Amen.

**Daughter Prays**

Heavenly Father, thank You for Your family.
You show love to all of Your children.
Help me to treat others right. It is no fun to be a "new kid."
Help my dad not to treat anyone at work like a "new kid." Amen.

How often *I* have longed
to gather your children together,
as a hen gathers her chicks
under her wings.

**MATTHEW 23:37**

It's 5:00 in the afternoon at a day care center not far from here. A little girl has been waiting for this moment since the first thing this morning. She stands at the windows, waiting for her daddy to drive into the parking lot. When the familiar car pulls in and the happy dad gets to the front door, those tiny legs can hardly move her fast enough to be smothered by a loving embrace.

God's love for us is just like this. He can be counted on to be there, and His surrounding arms fill us with the kind of happiness only a waiting child can know. It doesn't get any better than this.

### Dad Prays

Thank You, Heavenly Father, for Your embrace.

Thank You that I'm never too old to feel the safety of Your protection.

Forgive me for acting too big or too busy to fill my soul with Your love.

Give me an embracing affection for my family.

Please help my daughter to know the kind of love only You can give. Amen.

## Daughter Prays

Heavenly Father, thank You.
You hold me. You love me. You hear me.
Thank you that my dad loves me so much, too.
Help us to always hear each other and have great talks. Amen.

No *discipline seems pleasant at the time,*
*but painful. Later on, however,*
*it produces a harvest of righteousness and peace*
*for those who have been trained by it.*

**HEBREWS 12:11**

Planting seeds can be unrewarding work. When a farmer finishes
the task of placing thousands of tiny grains into the earth,
he can't even tell he's accomplished anything. But after a whole
summer of fertilizer and rain, his field produces a wonderful reward.

Doing the right thing can be a lot of thankless work. But God's
promise is that when we have done the hard work of planting seeds of
discipline in our lives, we will enjoy the fruit of righteousness and peace.

## Dad Prays

Thank You, Heavenly Father, for discipline.
Thank You for the rewards of obedience.
Forgive me for the times when I'm lazy or when I take
the easy way out, instead of doing what I know is right.
Please give my daughter the strength to be brave, and
please give her the joy of growing strong and true. Amen.

### Daughter Prays

Heavenly Father, thank You for guiding me.
I do not want to be lazy.
I want to do what is right.
Give my dad Your power.
We are glad when he wants to please You. Amen.

We also rejoice in our sufferings,
because we know that suffering produces perseverance;
perseverance, character;
and character, hope.

**ROMANS 5:3**

There is nothing quite like being on the winning team.
When the final buzzer goes off and the championship is won,
it's an awesome thing. What a celebration! However, winning almost
always comes from the discipline of practice, practice, and more practice.
Athletes who are willing to suffer the pain of practice
reap the rewards of victory.

When things don't exactly go our way, sometimes it really hurts.
But if we're patient and we don't give up, the rewards are
strong character and a hope for the future.

**Dad Prays**

Thank You, Heavenly Father, for pain.
Thank You because, when I am willing to face
the pain of discipline, my reward will be true happiness.
Forgive me for the times when I avoid pain and take the easy way.
Please help my daughter to be willing to face the pain of discipline
as she becomes the woman You created her to be. Amen.

**Daughter Prays**

Heavenly Father, sometimes pain is good.
Learning to do right is not easy.
But I want to do right and be happy.
Help me to work hard to learn.
And help my dad to set an example for us. Amen.

I *will instruct you and teach you*
*in the way you should go;*
I *will counsel you and watch over you.*

**PSALM 32:8**

Good dads are like good coaches. They tell their team how to play the game;
they make sure their players are in top physical condition.
They prepare them for the competition, then they watch
to be sure everything works properly.

God is a Good Father. His Word, the Bible, is filled with
clear instructions. He counts on our willingness to be disciplined.
He warns us of the craftiness of the opposition. Then He stands by,
lovingly making sure all goes according to His plan.
No wonder we love being members of His family.

**Dad Prays**

Thank You, Heavenly Father, for being a Wonderful Father.

Thank You for setting such a great example for me.

Forgive me when I fail to be the coach my family needs.

Please help my daughter to be an attentive student,

a disciplined person, and a godly woman. Amen.

## Daughter Prays

Heavenly Father, You set a great example.
*Help me to be the person that my family needs.*
*And help my dad to be a good coach for me.*
*Help him to show me who he wants me to be. Amen.*

Whoever can be trusted with
very little can also be trusted with much,
and whoever is dishonest with very little
will also be dishonest with much.
So if you have not been trustworthy
in handling worldly wealth,
who will trust you with true riches?

**L U K E   1 6 : 1 0 , 1 1**

Have you ever seen a smart baby? We hear proud dads and moms bragging about this a lot: "Look how she holds her head up." "See how her eyes are focusing?" So, if this baby is so smart, why don't her parents just go ahead and send her off to college? Now, isn't that a silly question?

Before a person can be trusted with college, she has to master high school. Before a person can be trusted with high school, she has to master middle school. Before a person can be trusted with big things, she has to master little things. This is one of life's most important truths.

## Dad Prays

Thank You, Heavenly Father, for trust.
Thank You for the things You have trusted me with.
Forgive me for thinking that I can have something
new before I take care of what I already have.
Please help my daughter to take good care of what she has
and not always want what she doesn't have. Amen.

## Daughter Prays

Heavenly Father, thank You for Your trust.
*Help me to take care of what I have.*
*And help my dad to take care of what he has. Amen.*

I do not run like a man running aimlessly;
I do not fight like a man beating the air.
No, I beat my body and make it my slave
so that after I have preached to others,
I myself will not be disqualified for the prize.

1 CORINTHIANS 9:26,27

Silver, gold, and platinum are very valuable. In fact, we call them "precious." The process precious metals go through to become valuable is called refining. They are heated until they melt; then impurities float to the surface and are removed. After they are cooled, they go through the fire again . . . and again . . . and again. None of this fire is enjoyable to these metals, but it's always worth it.

In order to become pure, you and I must go through the pain of discipline. We must learn how to say "no" to ourselves and how to do those things we know are good for us. Is this fun? No, but it's always worth it.

## Dad Prays

Thank You, Heavenly Father, for purity.
Thank You for the discipline I must go
through every day in order to become pure.
Forgive me for wanting the benefits of purity without
being willing to pay the price of self-discipline.
Please help my daughter to be pure. Amen.

## Daughter Prays

Heavenly Father, thank You for helping me to be clean inside.
I have to work every day to stay clean inside.
This is hard work. And it is good work.
Help my dad to be clean inside, too. Amen.

A cheerful heart is good medicine,
but a crushed spirit dries up the bones.

PROVERBS 17:22

Stop and think about your heart. Right now it's busily pumping gallons of blood through you. And it stays on the job every hour of every day. The blood your heart sends out carries wonderful things to your body—like good health and energy.

When we think joyful thoughts—like remembering the good things God has blessed us with—we are letting those thoughts pump through our spirits like life-giving blood. This gives our minds, our hearts, and even our bones lots of energy.

### Dad Prays

Thank You, Heavenly Father, for hope.
And thank You for giving us good things to think about.
Forgive me for the times when I become
discouraged and forget to let Your joy live in me.
Please fill my daughter with the good news of Your love.
And help her to know how much I love her, too. Amen.

**Daughter Prays**

Heavenly Father, thank You for hope.
*You give us good things to think about.*
*I want Your joy inside me.*
*Fill my dad with good thoughts.*
*Help him to be happy even when bad things happen. Amen.*

Whoever sows sparingly will also reap sparingly,
and whoever sows generously will also reap generously.
*Each man should give what*
*he has decided in his heart to give,*
*not reluctantly or under compulsion,*
*for God loves a cheerful giver.*

2 CORINTHIANS 9:6,7

Everybody loves birthdays, Christmas, and Father's Day—especially Father's Day! Why? Because people love to give and to receive gifts. These are always very happy times for our family.

It should come as no surprise that there is a direct connection between giving and happiness—when I am willing to look for ways to be generous toward others, the result will be personal satisfaction and joy. Having a giving spirit doesn't have to wait for a special day; it's something that can give us pleasure every day.

## Dad Prays

Thank You, Heavenly Father, for Your generosity.
Thank You for Your many, many gifts to me.
Forgive me for thinking that selfishness will bring me happiness.
Please help my daughter to have a giving heart.
Help her to experience the fun of being truly generous,
even with those who don't deserve it. Amen.

**Daughter Prays**

Heavenly Father, thank You for giving me so much.
You give me a lot of gifts.
Because of You, giving makes people feel good.
Help me to give.
And help my dad to give with a happy heart. Amen.

Rejoice in the Lord always.
I will say it again: Rejoice!

**PHILIPPIANS 4:4**

There are two kinds of people in the world: people who are
fun to be with and people who aren't. When people who aren't
fun to be with walk into a room, everyone holds their breath. But when
people who are fun to be with walk into a room, everyone celebrates.

Is our home a fun place to live? When people walk into our house,
are they glad to be there, or do they feel uncomfortable?
If our family is to be the kind of family that pleases God,
we don't have a choice in this matter. We need to have a happy home.

## Dad Prays

Thank You, Heavenly Father, for happiness.

Thank You for laughter, and thank You for happy homes.

Forgive me when I forget that it's my job to bring this happiness to our family.

Please help my daughter to also bring laughter and fun into our home. Amen.

**Daughter Prays**

Heavenly Father, thank You for making me happy.

*Thank You for making me laugh.*

*Thank You for my home.*

*Help me to do my part to make our home happy.*

*And help my dad to be happy even when he is thinking hard. Amen.*

$S$hout with joy to God, all the earth!

Sing the glory of his name;

make his praise glorious!

**PSALM 66:1, 2**

When a baseball player hits the winning home run . . . when
a basketball player sinks the winning free-throw . . . when a football player
catches the winning touchdown, everyone goes crazy. Happy screams,
hugging, and singing the school song are all part of this kind of celebration.

God wants us to live with joy. He wants to fill us with so many good things
that laughter and fun are just as ordinary as eating and sleeping.
Of course, our lives have plenty of serious moments, but
our family cannot forget to enjoy living, too.

## Dad Prays

Thank You, Heavenly Father, for celebration.
Thank You for the chance to fill our lives with laughter.
Forgive me when I take life too seriously.
Please help my daughter to enjoy life so much that
she brings that happiness into our home. Amen.

**Daughter Prays**

Heavenly Father, thank You for play.
Thank you for fun.
Help me to laugh and be happy.
Help my dad to have fun, too,
at football games and with our family. Amen.

You will go out in joy
and be led forth in peace;
the mountains and hills
will burst into song before you,
and all the trees of the field
will clap their hands.

ISAIAH 55:12

Encore! Encore! The concert has just finished and the applauding crowd is on its feet, begging the orchestra to come back for one more song. Everyone has been delighted by the performance. The happy smile on each person's face tells the story.

Our family should be like this—everyone is happy because of how well the orchestra played—and worked—together. Everybody did their part, and it was great. The mountains are humming a happy tune, and even the trees are applauding. There are few things more exciting than a standing ovation!

## Dad Prays

Thank You, Heavenly Father,
for Your applause—for Your incredible affirmation.
Thank You for giving us a family that can even make the trees of the fields
clap their hands with joy because of the joy we express to each other.
Forgive me when I forget to applaud loudly enough in our home.
I want to affirm my family every day.
Thank You for my daughter whom I love so much. Amen.

## Daughter Prays

Heavenly Father, thank You for the way
our family makes happy music together.
You put joy in our hearts.
I want to share Your joy with everyone.
Thanks for a dad with a happy heart. Amen.

$W$ithout faith it is impossible to please God,
because anyone who comes to him must believe that he exists
and that he rewards those who earnestly seek him.

**HEBREWS 11:6**

People go to school to learn. They want to learn as much as they can about everything, so they listen, read, and memorize the facts.

It is possible to learn a lot about our Creator. There are schools all over the world that help people to study as much as they can about Him. But knowing God—like you would know a good friend—only happens when we have faith. When we take the step from learning to believing, we truly discover who He is.

## Dad Prays

Thank You, Heavenly Father, for faith.
And thank You for giving me the ability to trust in Your plans for my life.
Forgive me for thinking that learning about You is
the same as having faith in You.
I want to love You and trust You.
Please fill my daughter with a love for You, too.
And teach her the joy of trusting in You as her friend. Amen.

**Daughter Prays**

Heavenly Father, thank You for showing me who You are.
I believe in You.
I love You and trust You.
Please help my dad to know You better all the time.
And help him to love You more and more, too. Amen.

Assemble the people before me to hear my words
so that they may learn to revere me
as long as they live in the land
and may teach them to their children.

DEUTERONOMY 4:10

There are crowds of people everywhere—shopping malls,
ball games, and concerts. And why are all these people together?
It's because something exciting is going on,
and they don't want to miss the action.

God commanded His people to gather together to listen to His voice.
It's not that people couldn't hear God's voice one at a time; it's that there was
something special about hearing His Word while surrounded by family and
friends. This is the reason our family goes to church. It's why you and I are
spending this time together. Somehow, when God speaks to more
than one person at a time, His voice is clearer.

## Dad Prays

Thank You, Heavenly Father, for Your Word.
*Thank You that when our whole family*
*hears it together, we hear it more clearly.*
*Forgive me when I forget how important it is*
*to gather together as a family to listen to You.*
*Please help my daughter to always value worshipping*
*You with her family and her friends. Amen.*

**Daughter Prays**

Heavenly Father, thank You for teaching us.
I hear You clearly.
And I learn so much.
It is good to learn when my family is together.
Help my dad do this. Amen.

Let us then approach the throne of grace with confidence,
so that we may receive mercy
and find grace to help us in our time of need.

**HEBREWS 4:16**

When a king enters a room, common people are required to bow down
out of humility and respect. Sometimes the royal person acknowledges
the ordinary people, and sometimes he completely ignores them.
What he does is totally up to him. This has been true for thousands of years.

Our God welcomes us into His presence. And even though we are
overwhelmed with awe and respect for who He is, our Father asks us
to come to Him boldly. Then, not only does He recognize us as
His loyal subjects, He grants us His mercy and calls us His own children.
This has been true since the beginning of time, and it will be true forever.

### Dad Prays

Thank You, Heavenly Father, for mercy.

Thank You that even though You are the King of kings,

You mercifully call me Your son.

Forgive me for apologizing for myself in Your presence.

Give me boldness.

Please help my daughter to live in the joy of knowing

that You also love her as your very own daughter. Amen.

Daughter Prays

Heavenly Father, thank You for Your kindness.
You are the King of kings.
But You call me Your child.
Please give my dad the courage to tell others about his love for You. Amen.

Godliness with contentment is great gain.
For we brought nothing into the world,
and we can take nothing out of it.
But if we have food and clothing,
we will be content with that.

1  T I M O T H Y   6 : 6 - 8

Our favorite waitress came to our table with a fresh pot of coffee.
Dad already had a bunch of cups, so he said, "I'll just take a half a cup."
As our waitress started to pour, she said to Dad,
"Say 'when.'" Too late. The cup was already full.

It's so easy to want more than we have. Sometimes it's hard to not feel jealous
when someone has something we wish we could have—or to know when
to say, "when." God graciously meets our physical needs, but best of all,
He lavishly pours out His love. Thank You, Father; Your love is enough.

Dad Prays

Thank You, Heavenly Father, for enough.

Thank You for giving our family the basics . . . and so much more.

Forgive me for forgetting how very rich I am.

Even though it's hard not to want more, please help my daughter to be

thankful for what she has, especially because she has You. Amen.

## Daughter Prays

Heavenly Father, thank You for giving us so much.

*We have what we need to be happy.*

*My dad works hard.*

*He buys food for us.*

*He provides a place for us to live.*

*I am thankful for all that I have.*

*Help my dad to know how glad we are.*

*Help him to be happy because he has You. Amen.*

It is the LORD your God you must follow,
and him you must revere.
Keep his commands and obey him;
serve him and hold fast to him.

**DEUTERONOMY 13:4**

If we were going backpacking in the woods, we would want to bring along plenty of provisions: food, warm clothing, medicine, something to sleep on, and a compass. We would need these things when we got hungry, cold, sick, tired, or lost. But of all these things, our compass is the most important, because it guides us to the right path.

Some people think they can go on a trip without asking directions. Dads are especially good at this. But people who try to go through life without God's guidance usually find themselves as lost as a backpacker without a compass. What a frightening thing that would be.

## Dad Prays

Thank You, Heavenly Father, for directions.
Thank You for giving me Yourself—Someone I can follow.
Forgive me for the times when I fail to ask You
for directions, thinking that I know what's best.
Please help my daughter learn how to trust
You and how to follow You, too. Amen.

**Daughter Prays**

Heavenly Father, thank You for showing me which way to go.
I am glad that I can follow You.
I am glad that I can trust You when
I am unsure about what I should do.
Help my dad to trust You for directions, too. Amen.

When you pray,
do not keep on babbling like pagans,
for they think they will be heard
because of their many words.
Do not be like them,
for your Father knows what you need before you ask him.

**MATTHEW 6:7, 8**

"Wow, Dad, how did you know?" the happy girl squealed
as she finished tearing off the pretty wrapping paper. "This is just
what I wanted!" Anyone can buy a gift for someone that's right off
their what-I-want-for-Christmas gift list, but it takes someone
special to know exactly what to give, without the list.

God our Father knows what we want. Sure, He wants us to tell Him,
but He doesn't need for us to beg. He knows what is best.
In fact, He knows so well that sometimes when we "open"
what He has given us, we're not sure if we like it.
But later on, we understand what He had in mind.

## Dad Prays

Thank You, Heavenly Father, for Your gifts.
Thank You for knowing exactly what I need,
even if it's something that I don't think I want!
Forgive me for foolishly begging You, forgetting
that You already know what is best for me.
Please help my daughter to trust You to give her what she truly needs. Amen.

**Daughter Prays**

Heavenly Father, thank You for all that You give to me.

I do not have to beg.

You simply know what I need.

You want the best for me, even when

I do not know what the best is.

You help my dad, too.

Help him to know that. Amen.

Whether you eat or drink
or whatever you do,
do it all for the glory of God.

1 CORINTHIANS 10:31

Birds sing their songs, and trees stand tall. Strong rivers flow to the sea, and flowers bloom in pallets of vibrant color. God gave them each a job to do, and they do those jobs to the best of their ability! And even though obeying God is all they know, it still makes Him happy when birds, trees, rivers, and flowers do these things.

People can make a choice about how they act. But God has put in our hearts the ability to do things right. When we do what we ought to do and we give it our very best, that pleases Him. It also makes us happy when we choose to obey.

### Dad Prays

Thank You, Heavenly Father, for Your ways.

And thank You for giving me the choice of being obedient to You.

Forgive me for the times when I go my own way, disobeying You.

Please remind my daughter that choosing to follow You is always best.

And help me to be a good example for her to follow. Amen.

**Daughter Prays**

Heavenly Father, thank You for letting me choose how to live my life.
I do not want to go my own way.
I want to obey You.
Help my dad to make the right choices
even when it is hard. Amen.

Remind the people to be subject to rulers and authorities,
to be obedient, to be ready to do whatever is good,
to slander no one, to be peaceable and considerate,
and to show true humility toward all men.

TITUS 3:1, 2

No one can see the wind. It's completely invisible. But everyone can see what the wind does. When it's blowing softly, the trees gently sway in its breeze. And when it becomes a tornado, its power to destroy is frightening.

People's character—what's inside of them—is also invisible. But just as we see the effects of the wind, we see the outside effects of people's character everywhere. Our conduct—the way we act— can be a gentle breeze, soothing and comforting others, or it can be a windstorm, hurting everyone in its path.

## Dad Prays

Thank You, Heavenly Father, for the wind.
Thank You for reminding me that what I do comes from who I am.
Please help my daughter to be the woman You want her to be.
Then please help her to show others, like her family and her friends,
who she is by her obedience to You and her kindness toward them. Amen.

**Daughter Prays**

Heavenly Father, thank You for the wind.
The wind reminds me that what I do reflects who I am.
This is true for my dad, too.
Please fill my dad with Your Spirit.
Help him to be the man You want him to be.
Help him to be tender.
And help him to be humble. Amen.

Whatever is true, whatever is noble,
whatever is right, whatever is pure,
whatever is lovely, whatever is admirable—
if anything is excellent or praiseworthy—
think about such things.

**PHILIPPIANS 4:8**

Before an airplane can take off, the flight attendants must tell everyone
how to use their oxygen masks. They tell us that if something
bad happens while we're airborne, we might have a hard time breathing.
Without oxygen we would cough and choke. Fortunately,
the plane is ready with lots of good, clean air to breathe.

What we think about is like the air. If our minds are not filled with
good things, our spirits will sputter and die. Filling our minds with
clean things is like taking a gulp of fresh air. How wonderful it is that
God's Word has a huge supply of good things to think about.

## Dad Prays

Thank You, Heavenly Father, for my mind.
Thank You for the choice I have to fill my mind with good things.
Forgive me when I don't think about noble, pure, and admirable things.
Even though my daughter hears a lot of bad things,
please help her to always think about lovely things. Amen.

**Daughter Prays**

Heavenly Father, thank You for my mind.
You let me fill my mind with good things.
Make my dad strong.
Help him to think only good and clean thoughts. Amen.

*Consecrate yourselves and be holy,*
*because I am the LORD your God.*
*Keep my decrees and follow them.*
*I am the LORD, who makes you holy.*

**LEVITICUS 20:7, 8**

The sign reads, "Wet paint. Do not touch." When some people see that sign, they think they must touch the paint, just to be sure the sign isn't kidding. If we look carefully at the fresh paint, we can always tell if someone touched it. Their fingerprints are there for good.

God commands us to be holy. This means that we are to be like fresh paint—perfect, without any fingerprints! But without God's forgiveness, this would be impossible. His grace is like a fresh coat of paint that gives us a new start every day— a new chance to be holy because He is holy.

## Dad Prays

Thank You, Heavenly Father, for holiness.
Thank You for Your grace that gives me
a fresh start every day—a new chance to be holy.
Forgive me for giving up when the challenge to be holy seems unreachable.
Please help my daughter to live in the beauty of Your forgiveness every day. Amen.

**Daughter Prays**

Heavenly Father, thank You for being holy.

*Every day I have a fresh start.*

*Every day I have a new chance to live a good life.*

*I do not want to give up.*

*I want to keep trying.*

*Help my dad to live a holy life, too. Amen.*

A man reaps what he sows. . . .
Let us not become weary in doing good,
for at the proper time we will reap a harvest
if we do not give up.

**GALATIANS 6:7,9**

What kinds of food would we prefer not to be served at dinner? Okra? Eggplant? Asparagus? Broccoli? Let's say that we prepared a garden in our back yard and then took a trip to our favorite hardware store to buy seeds. Would we buy and plant seeds for any of the things we didn't like? Of course we wouldn't.

One of the most important principles in all of life is that you and I "harvest" what we "plant." Doing honest, kind, fair, and good things day after day helps us to grow into the kind of person we really want to be—the kind of person who pleases God.

## Dad Prays

Thank You, Heavenly Father, for planting and reaping.

Thank You for this very important truth—

that what I sow in my life, I will also harvest.

Forgive me for forgetting that what I do soon becomes who I am.

Please help my daughter to remember to always plant good seeds. Amen.

## Daughter Prays

Heavenly Father, thank You for seeds and crops.
I plant a seed and it grows.
And what grows, I can pick.
In the same way, what I do becomes who I am.
Help my dad to remember to plant good seeds. Amen.

## About the Author

**Robert Wolgemuth** is a speaker and the author of several books, including *She Calls Me Daddy: Seven Things Every Man Needs to Know About Building a Complete Daughter,* and the notes for *The Devotional Bible for Dads* by Zondervan. *The Portable She Calls Me Daddy,* published by Honor Books. His monthly column, "Hey, Dad!" is featured in *HomeLife Magazine.* Robert is also the founder of Wolgemuth & Associates, Inc., a literary representation agency.

An elder in the Presbyterian Church (USA), Robert teaches a Sunday school class with more than 400 members. He and his wife, Bobbie, have two adult daughters, a son-in-law, and two precious grandchildren.

This and other titles by Robert Wolgemuth are available
from your local bookstore.

*She Calls Me Daddy,* Trade
*She Calls Me Daddy,* Portable
*The Devotional Bible for Dads*

Honor Books
Tulsa, Oklahoma